# Keep Your Hopes Up High

# And Your Head Down Low:

## A Compilation

By P.W. Francis Schwille

PWFS Printing, New York

ISBN: 978-1481118439

Published by PWFS Printing, New York

Cover Illustration by Jacob Premo

Edited By: Krysten Marie Beck & Angela Cerbone

Printed in the United States of America

# Table of Contents

I would like to thank my friends, family, and teachers. You have all been my mentors and all have been my inspiration.

My friends and family mean the world to me. This book, my first of hopefully many, is dedicated to all of you and to my forever best friend, Francis "Frankie" Garguilo. I can never and will never forget you.

"Regret nothing; Live Life to it's Fullest!"

– Krysten Marie Beck

Introduction

"Let the things that hurt you fuel you to become stronger in the end." These have become the words that I live by, my motto. They serve to remind me I can do *this* regardless of others, occurrences, or even times that have said otherwise—and many of you can vouch for the thick-headedness which calls for this comment—myself.

Yet, in spite of *them* and *me*, I have here, my first published compilation of poems. They share what goes on in my head, what I hold in there; they stand as proverbial passwords to my mind. You are always on my mind, good friends, and, even more so, you are in these poems. You have helped me to *keep my hopes up high and my head down low*. And for this, I will certainly be forever grateful.

## Don't Fret My Friend

Don't fret my friend
for you are loved.
When you hurt,
I hurt.
When you cry,
I cry.
My goal is to keep you happy,
to keep you smiling,
to keep you being you.
For I am your protector,
your guardian,
your brother.
Don't fret my friend
for I will always be with you.

## Inexcusable

You broke her heart
and that is inexcusable.
Forgiveness is something I cannot give you.
Mercy is something you do not deserve.
Who knows what would happen if our paths crossed again.
Right now I am calm
but the beast is waiting to erupt.
I must thank you though
for if this had not occurred
then she would have never found her true friends.
I warn you again
if we meet and if there is a God
so help you!
You better begin to pray
as I draw near.

## A Dream

To hold you tight
is a dream of mine.
I yearn to be loved,
to love somebody.
Shall we end this game?
I am sick of this.
We play and play
and questions arise.
We must stop teasing each other
and be open with one another.
Let your feelings go, My Love!
And I will too!
Finally we will be together.

## Hold You Close

Whether near or far,
close or distant,
you will always have a special place in my heart.
When you weep,
I weep.
When you're frustrated,
I'm frustrated.
Your happiness is all I care about
and I always do my best to make sure of it.
I hold you close in my mind and my heart
and that will never cease to be.

# Earth-Shaker

He couldn't be held back anymore.
The people are running.
This beast has had enough,
he's been walked over for the last time.

They once revered him,
once adored him,
once worshiped him,

but then they disgraced him,
ruined him,
maimed him.

She left him,
laughed at him,
mocked him.

And for all of this,
you will all pay.

His time for revenge is now,
he's coming back to avenge the injustice,
back to bring the apocalypse.

You will all beg for mercy,
when I come back.
I will stand over you as you remain on your knees,
I will look into your eyes,
stare at your tears,
and I will laugh.

# A Man Apart

I am torn,
a man apart.
I love you,
but you don't love me.
You tease me
with your beauty.
You drive me wild
when you play with your hair.
You are a forbidden fruit,
the one that everyone wants.
A hug and a kiss
is my limit with you.

My arm around you
feels so good
but you keep up your guard.
We are closer than ever
but that's where we stand…

Drop your shields,
my love.
I offer you everything I can:
warmth when my arms are around you,
a tight hug,
a gentle kiss,
sweet words.

## For So Long

We've known each other for so long
or it feels like so long.
We've never been closer
than we are now.
This special bond we share
that cannot be broken.
Through good
we've grown close.
Through bad
we've grown even closer.
I need not write this
but am compelled to
for words are how I express myself best
to you and to the world.

# Standing Here

I've walked these lines,
through smoke and fire,
for miles and miles,
I've been to hell and back.

The soul is gone,
and my life is not mine.
These things I did for you to see,
before you took the leap…

Here I stand,
a broken mess.
All alone tonight,
and I wish I was strong enough to do this deed,
to breathe without you by my side.

# The City, My City

My city yearns to be loved
with its bright lights and busy streets
and I do love thee.
For my city holds my loved ones
all nestled together,
waiting for their savior.

My city yearns to be hated
and I do hate it
with its many people and its noise at all hours.
It makes me insane
like I've lost all control sometimes.

The city is like my brother,
my sister,
my lover,
my son,
my daughter.

I love this city,
MY city.
But why am I here?
Why does my city call my name?
Do I have a purpose?
Am I the one to save my city?
Am I its savior?
It's Superman?

## I Will Say No

Again and again
you under estimate my power.
But the day will come
when I let loose with rage.
You will not be able to withstand my awesome might.
I will stand over you.
You will beg for mercy.
and I will say no.

## Have You Ever Thought

Have you ever stood in front of a fire and thought:
I wonder what it would be like to burn?
Have you ever sat in a car and thought:
I wonder what it would be like to hit something?
Have you ever stood on a cliff and thought:
If I just jumped right now, would anyone give a damn?
Have you ever held a gun in your hand and thought:
If I just put this to my head and pulled the trigger then all
the crap would be forgotten?
Have you ever had a day where you thought:
Maybe I should just drink myself to death?

Have you ever thought these things?
Cause I have…

1

May I take your hand now and make you mine
for you are beautiful and perfect here.
You are as radiant as the sunshine.
Through all seasons you bring sunshine to me.
Through all my dark times you stayed by my side.
Just the thought of you keeps me warm inside.
My love for you will be never ending
like my love for a favorite sports team.
Through thick and thin our love will remain strong.
Fueled by your love I will overcome all.
All obstacles will now be easy with you
by my side I feel like your superman.
   I will never love someone as I you;
   my little lady, my girl forever.

2

You are as radiant as the sunshine.
In all my dark times I looked to you there.
I would never dream of stopping that shine.
You are too perfect to be with me here.
Thoughts of you always keep me warm inside.
You are beautiful and petite to me.
Through all my dark times you stayed by my side.
I just hope that someday you too will see,
you are the scorn of many a woman.
They look at you with contempt in their eyes
with you here I feel like your superman.
Sometimes the looks you give leave me in ties.
      So I would never want to make you mine
      because you know that too big is my spine.

3

What beauty can I speak of
that hasn't been said in the past?
You are like a dove
that should be in another caste.
You are the envy of many women
with your blue eyes and blonde hair.
You are the "gold" for all men
because you should be royalty or an heir.
Being your enemy would be foolish of any man
I will never be that stupid.
I would much rather be your hero, your superman.
If only I am lucky enough to get an arrow from cupid.
       Through many of my worst times you were here
       I only wish that I could always do the same for you there.

4

You are as beautiful as a sunrise,
or a flower in bloom.
And you are so wise,
you brighten up any room.
I yearn to be your superman
though I know the chances are narrow.
I will fight any man
if only I could find an arrow.
I wish that I could show you how much to me you mean.
You are the apple of my eye.
I wish that could be seen.
I never want to say goodbye.
   You deserve all that you desire
   and I will do all that is required.

When I look at you,
I want you to be mine.
If only you felt this way too,
if only you'd give me a sign.
Let me be your superman,
let me show you how much you mean to me.
I will fight any man,
if only you could see,
just what I would do for you.
Let me show you how I feel,
I promise that I will be true.
I want to be your man of steel.
What's this that I speak of?
I believe it to be love.

## 6 or To My Best Friend

Allow me to open up my heart,
allow me to speak
For you were so kind to me right from the start.
only honesty is what we seek.
You were there for me through quite a low
that's something I can only dream of repaying you for.
Your presence in my life has certainly helped me to grow
and that is something that I will not ignore.
You are one of the most beautiful girls I have ever seen,
it is certainly a pleasure to call you my best friend.
To think of you not in my life would be obscene,
it is nothing I would recommend.

       You are in a whole other category, you are a dove,
       and all I have for you is love.

## Hope

When the cards of life were shrewd about
when I lost all hope,
had my doubts,
you threw a rope
and made me believe again
in the strength of a friend.
When most of life, I've lived in vain
you came through to help mend,
my life, which stood for downfall
though you were unaware.
I was on my hands and knees, beginning to crawl.
It was a burden I was willing to bear.
       Thanks aren't enough, for you.
       You are owed much more, this is true.

## 8 or Another Late Night

Should daddy's little girl be out this late?
Strolling and searching for what is right.
She'll certainly be in danger at this rate
for she can't withstand the darkness' might.
She's gagged and she's bound
What else could go wrong?
What else has she found?
The demons begin to write their song.
The world will now know
as the tears now set in
that if you see the black crow
get ready for sin.
        But when I arrive, all will be well.
        She will be safe, the one who fell.

Right from the beginning you were a friendly face
you taught me so much.
I knew I was in a good place
and we went as such.
But then one night
when all the cards came unfold
I picked up my tools and began to write,
the chance was now rolled.
I never imagined what was to come
how our friendship grew
how can I come to sum:
It's all so true.
        Our friendship may be new
        But I love you, darling, that I do.

## 10 or The One On My Mind

Each day of mine you brighten.
The thought of your keeps me warm.
Each day we speak, our bond is tightened,
I can't wait to hold you through a storm.
It hurts sometimes to see you there
standing so beautifully with that cute stare
and not be able to show you I care.
I wish to kiss you, I do dare.
To have and to hold you is a dream.
To shout it from the roof
just how much you mean
would be the proper proof.
       The day will come where we will finally have our chance to be.
       I yearn for you, if only the world could see.

## A Burden

When I hurt someone I care about
I hurt myself.
You may think I don't care
but that is the furthest thing from the truth.
The last thing on my mind is to harm you.
I'd rather hurt myself than the ones around me
Yet I always seem to hurt them first.

It must be a burden I bear,
to always be a screw up.
To always build others up
and then unintentionally bring them down.
Much like I am down.

It is something I am still learning,
something I am still confused by,
something I must fix.

# Be Gone!

Get out of my life!
Be gone from me!
You've tortured me with your crap for far too long.
I hate everything about you,
everything that is you.
Why do I still feel this urge to be near you?
Once I loved you,
But now all I feel is anger.
Be gone from me!
The torture you inflicted is over!

# The Way I Feel

The way you make me feel

like the happiest guy on the planet.

My life prospects looked so bleak

and my future so dim.

But then you entered my world

and things took a turn.

Happiness has overcome me.

Joy, overwhelmed me.

Stress has flew out the window

and I have begun to take life in stride.

There is never enough that I could say to thank you for this.

I could shout it from the rooftops

though that wouldn't be enough.

Thank you for being you

and thank you for loving me.

## You Stand There

When we met I had no idea
how I would come to feel about you.
You stand there without a clue
as to how I really feel.

If only it was easy to speak my mind
but words are my release.
I could write about you for days and days
but I could never express myself properly through speech.

Life is so frustrating
and you make it feel so much better.
A soft laugh,
an adorable smile,
and my day is complete.

## Where am I?

Here I lay
down on this soft bed.
I like it
for it is cozy,
comfortable some may say.
But now it is dark,
It is confiding,
engulfing,
tight.
No I don't like this at all.
I am dressed well though,
suit and tie.
Not what I normally wear to sleep.
Where am I?
Heaven?
Hell?
Am I dreaming?
Am I dead?
Where am I?

# A Ghost on the Canvas

What has he become?
Who is he anymore?
Please tell him
because he has no idea anymore.
He is a ghost on the canvas,
waiting for someone to bring him back to life.

He's let too much negative overwhelm him,
engulf him,
complete him,
make up his entire being for far too long.

He does not know who is…

It's time I came back.
It's time I stood strong.
Not knowing who I am solves nothing.
This ghost on the canvas is ready to be redrawn,
ready to be whole again.

## Miles Away

If you only knew just how much you meant to me.
You were my friend,
my brother.

But now you're miles away
and I wish I could talk to you right now,
tell you all the things that I've seen.

Nobody knows the real me,
sometimes I just want to scream.
I often look to you for solace
but you're no longer here.

As I grow older now,
I fear for my life.
As the days go by,
I would kill for a chance to drive,
to get away from here and find you there,
and tell you of my life.

Though my time has been so little
it's been a long road so far.
There's no turning back from here,
no more dwelling on my fears.

## I Walk
### (Relay for Life)

One second I had you and life was grand
the next it took you from me.
Some would lose all hope, fall down, and give up
but I chose to walk.
I walk for all those out there in need of love.
I walk for those in need of company.
I walk for friends,
for brothers,
for sisters,
for husbands,
for wives,
for grandmothers,
for grandfathers,
for aunts,
for uncles,
for cousins.
I walk so that one day I will not have to.
I walk for you.
I walk for me.
I walk for a cure.

## Shed No Tear

Have no fear

and shed no tear.

This is not a goodbye forever

but merely a "see you soon."

This new chapter we will start soon will be hard and stressing

but if anyone can overcome it,

it is us.

Times will be tough

but remain steadfast

like I know you can.

Though you don't think so,

when you are sad,

I am sad.

When I hurt you,

I hurt myself.

I'm not the smartest guy

and I don't know much

but I do know that I adore you.

# I Just Don't Know

I just don't know what to do.
Life is full of ups and downs.
There is never a happy medium.

One point I'm down and out,
depressed and hurt.

The next, I'm happy and great,
excited and overjoyed.

Then I'm back to down and out,
punching walls, bleeding knuckles,
being the hurter and hurting myself.

I just don't know what to do,
I just don't.

## A Land of Darkness

This world has taken all it can from me
and has left me in shambles.
My blood is as cold as ice
or so I have been told.
I show no emotion
and it has destroyed my soul.
I now enjoy the ride
on this train wreck called life.
I'm in a land of darkness
from which I cannot return.

## You

It happened by surprise but it was always there.

Now I can't get you out of my mind.

I catch a scent and think of you.

I see a place and I see you.

I look to challenges and see you next to me.

I close my eyes and see you in my arms.

## All Gave Some, Some Gave All

On this day there is so much you could say.
We lost so many good people on this day.
I was just a child then
but the hurt is all the same.
Years later I may be stronger and older
but I still get a lump in my throat and a tear in my eye
when I think about what occurred.

Lives may have been lost but our pride was found.
We continue to live our lives
letting all those know that even the worst
will not put us down.
Those heroes didn't die so that we would give up.
Let the things that hurt you,
fuel you to become stronger in the end.
ALL gave some,
Some gave ALL.
But we will never forget any of you.

## Open the Book

Some stories you want to finish.

Some you wish would never end.

Some you want to shut tight

and others you never want to close.

But when all is said and done don't you want to be able to say that you picked up the book?

Made in the USA
Middletown, DE
06 November 2023

41876768R00029